The Street Names
of Hitchin

and Their Origins

Book 1: The Town Centre

Sue Fitzpatrick
and
Barry West

EGON

EGON PUBLISHERS LTD

End papers: *Map of Hitchin by Drapentier, 1700*
Title page: *Portrait of a Hitchin Pedestrian by Samuel Lucas*
Below: *Carriage entrance to Sun Hotel, Sun Street.*
Page 3: *Door knocker, Roslyn House, Sun Street.*
Page 5: *Plaster wreath, Sun Street.*

Copyright © Egon Publishers Limited and
Hitchin Historical Society, 1997

ISBN 1 899998 25 X

Designed by
Nick Maddren, Campion Publishing Services, Baldock,
Hertfordshire, SG7 6BD
for Egon Publishers Limited

Printed in England by
Streets Printers, Royston Road, Baldock, Hertfordshire, SG7 6NW

Foreword

For some years Sue Fitzpatrick and I had been considering the production of a booklet on the origins of Hitchin's road names and had begun researching and writing to that end. Following her tragic death at the end of 1995, I resolved to finish the work we had begun together as a small memorial to Sue and her enthusiasm for the history of my home town. In this book both visitors and lifelong residents alike will, I hope, find something of interest, whether indoors on a cold winter's night or walking around these very streets, book in hand.

It had become apparent that to include every road in one book would be a mammoth task so, in consultation with other members of the Hitchin Historical Society, I have decided to divide the town into areas with a separate publication for each. This is the first, covering the geographical centre of Hitchin. Others will follow as circumstances permit. I have defined the central area as that encompassed by Highbury Road, St. John's Road, Park Way, Old Park Road, Bedford Road, Fishponds Road, Bunyan Road, Nightingale Road and Verulam Road.

I cannot guarantee that there are no errors whatsoever in the work or that all the relevant information has been found. The subject would repay much more detailed research into primary sources which time has not permitted. If any reader has any knowledge to add I should be extremely grateful if it could be communicated to the Hitchin Historical Society, either directly or through Hitchin Museum, so that it may be incorporated in any future edition.

My thanks must go to everyone who has had any part in the preparation and publication of this booklet. Full acknowledgements appear later, and I here apologise for any omissions. There are still two more parts of the work to come and I hope and trust that this support and help will continue to be made available.

Barry West
Hitchin, 1997

In Memoriam

Sue Fitzpatrick

She is dead, the little mother sparrow
with the twittering fingers and the narrow flame
shooting up her spine like an intolerable arrow,
   but things go on much the same.

To be dead is just another stage of forgetting.
Small distant lightnings in a distant field
will dance on regardless, the sun continue setting:
   nothing's permanently healed.

But to be finished, thereby setting off events
in darkness is too terrible for words
that are only movements, brittle sacraments,
   thin flights of scrawking birds.

Look, I can set them in motion by waving a pen
across paper or by breathing on a glass
and drawing with fingers then wiping clean again
   like turning off the gas.

She's dead, sweet little sparrow, and I cannot claim
to have loved her or known her well or said
anything of comfort or use, but write down her name
   for safekeeping now she is dead.

George Szirtes

Hitchin

Hitchin first appears as *Hicca* in the *Tribal Hidage,* a seventh century document listing Anglo-Saxon tribes. Although not numerous the Hicce tribe controlled an area extending to about a six or seven mile radius of the modern town. In the eighth century, when King Offa of Mercia was extending his kingdom, the Hitchin Gap in the Chilterns was of strategic importance in the push south-eastwards and it is probably from this time that the area can trace its royal links.

The *Domesday Book* of 1086 refers to the manor as Hiz, the name by which the river is known today. It would appear, however, that this was a Norman French spelling and that the pronunciation of the name continued to be 'hitch', with the 'in' ending appearing over time to become the modern version.

Although there is evidence of Roman and earlier occupation of the area and the name *Highbury* suggests a possible fortified settlement on the high ground overlooking the modern town, its foundation can quite likely be traced to the establishment of the monastery on the site of the present parish church in 792. A market would have quickly become established at the monastery gate, leading to settlement around it. Hitchin seems never to have achieved full borough status despite one reference to 'the borough' but topographical evidence indicates that urban plots of land were deliberately laid out along Bancroft, Bucklersbury and Sun Street.

Over the centuries Hitchin grew slowly. Back Street, Bridge Street and Tilehouse Street became established away from the market, and the large market place itself was infilled in parts with islands of buildings. The next great change, however, came following the construction of the railway station in 1850 a mile away in what were then open fields. The town grew out to meet the railway. Artisans' and workers' dwellings were erected between Nightingale and Walsworth Roads, whilst the middle classes preferred the higher ground of the Nettledell Estate to the south. Some expansion was taking place in other directions but, essentially, the next large growth of Hitchin did not come until shortly before and after the Second World War.

Bridge Street. Drawing by Frederick L Griggs.

An asterisk denotes a name no longer in use. The dates in italics are of recorded references in documents or on maps.

Adam and Eve Alley took its name from the *Adam and Eve* public house in Bancroft, now existing in a rebuilt form as the *Tut 'n' Shive*. It is sometimes known as Bunyan Path since it leads from Bancroft to Bunyan Road. *1861*

Allen's Yard* - see Bennett's Yard. *1851*

Angel Street* - see Sun Street. *1713, Angell Street 1676, 1700*

Arcade Walk - see The Arcade

Aram's Alley* - see Munt's Alley.

Back Street* - see Queen Street. *1676, 1700, 1818, 1841, 1844, 1851, 1861*

Baldock Road* - see Nightingale Road and Walsworth Road. *1844*

Bancroft has been known at times as Bancroft Street, and is believed to have taken its name from a bean croft, or field where beans were grown. A survey of 1557 refers to 'the bean market', showing how important the crop had become. The street follows approximately the line of the minor Roman road from Verulamium (St. Albans) to Sandy and the northern part was at one time called Silver Street, a name which seems to be associated with Roman roads. The southern end has, in the recent past, been commonly known as Moss's Corner after the grocery business of W.B. Moss and Sons which occupied premises at its junction with the High Street, on the site of the *Trooper* public house.

Baroque porch, The Croft, Bancroft by Gerard Ceunis.

Top: *Plaque, Bancroft.*
Above: *Courtyard of the Manor House, Bancroft.*

Earlier, though, this end and its link to the Churchyard had been called Golden Square, originally Gilden Square, after the Guildhouse of the Brotherhood of Our Lady, which existed from 1475 until its dissolution by King Henry VIII's commissioners in 1548. The building still survives in an altered form adjacent to Lloyds Bank. There is evidence that at one time a market cross stood nearby and, until the beginning of the twentieth century, the sheep and cattle market was held here. Sometimes, one finds the name Bancroft also being used to include the present High Street. *1676, 1700, 1818, 1844, 1851, 1861, 1879*

Bancroft Street* - see Bancroft. *1532, 1534, 1676, 1841, 1897, Bancroftstret 1460, 1475*

Barnard's Yard* was one of the yards to the west of Queen Street which disappeared in the 1920s slum clearance. In 1851 there was an Arthur Barnard, a rag and bone dealer, and a Thomas Barnard, marine store dealer, both living in Bridge Street. *1851, 1861, 1880, 1891*

Bedford Road is the road to Bedford. *1879*

Bennett's Yard* was a yard off Bancroft, earlier known as Allen's Yard, which probably took its name from Thomas Bennett, a whitesmith. *1861*

Bethel Lane* - see St. John's Road. *1844, 1851, 1883, 1891*

Bethel Path* - see St. John's Path. *1891*

Biggin Lane takes its name from the building known as *The Biggin*, the successor to the Gilbertine Priory of New Bigging which existed here from 1361 until 1538. *1676, 1700, 1841, 1844, 1851, 1861, 1880*

The Biggin by Gerard Ceunis.

Brand Street was originally much narrower than it is now and was called Pound Lane because it led to the pound where stray animals were impounded. It also seems to have been known as Pulter's Lane and may be the Park Lane referred to in a survey of 1676. It was widened in 1834 and renamed Broad Street, as shown on an 1844 map, although the 1841 census refers to it by its present name, which arose because Sir Thomas Brand was the Member of Parliament for Hertfordshire at the time. This name was officially confirmed by the Local Board of Health in 1852. *1841, 1861, 1880*

Bridge Street is obviously named from the bridge over the River Hiz, the present one being dated 1784 although 'the Bridgefoot' is mentioned in a 1676 survey. The street had earlier been known as Spital or Spittle Street because it led to Spital Field, one of the mediaeval open fields of the town. This, in turn, took its name from the Pesthouse or Hospital which stood within it. Part of Bridge Street has also been known as Bull Street, and the wide junction with the other roads at its eastern end as Bull Corner. It has been suggested that bull-baiting as a popular form of entertainment took place here, and there was once a public house of that name in the street. Bull Corner later became known as The Triangle because of a railed off triangular area of land at the road junction upon which an

Nos 8, 9 and 9A Bridge Street

9

acacia tree grew. *1676, 1818, 1841, 1844, 1851, 1880, Brydgestrete 1546, Bridgestreate 1546, 1556*

Bristow's Yard* took its name from Whiston Bristow, who ran a school at his Bancroft house in the early nineteenth century, where he lived with his wife, Judith, and their five children, two pupil teachers, eleven pupils, a male servant and a female servant with her baby daughter. *1841, 1851*

Broad Street* - see Brand Street. *1844*

Brooker's Yard - see Exchange Yard.

Nos 17 and 18 Bucklersbury

Bucklersbury has a name which, apart from differences in spelling, has not changed over the centuries, but for which no explanation has been found. It has been suggested that it originally meant the armourers' quarter, but it seems unlikely that Hitchin ever had a large number of armourers working here. A buckler might also have been a harness maker, however. There is a Bucklersbury in the City of London which, it is believed, may derive from a personal or family name. If the same explanation were accepted here, it still begs the question of whether bury implies a fortified enclosure in this area. *1676, 1818, 1841, 1844, 1851, 1880, Bucklers Bury 1700, Bucklers berye 1591*

Bull Corner* - see Bridge Street. *1700, 1844, 1851*

Bull Street* - see Bridge Street. *1676, Bullestrete 1546*

10

Bunyan Path - see Adam and Eve Alley.

Bunyan Road is a nineteenth century street, probably taking its name from John Bunyan of Elstow, the author of *Pilgrim's Progress*. His aunt Alice, the daughter of Thomas Bunyan, lived in Hitchin for many years, being buried in St. Mary's churchyard in 1614. Bunyan's sister, Elizabeth, was also baptized here in 1638. *1879, 1882*

Butterfield's Yard* was a Bancroft yard, once occupied by W. and H. Butterfield, contractors and builders. *1861*

Cannon's Yard* was a yard off Queen Street, presumably named after its owner or occupier. *1891*

Cemetery Path is so called because it leads from Hollow Lane to the Standhill Road gate of the cemetery.

Cemetery Road* - see Standhill Road. *1870, 1880*

Cemetery Road passes between the new and older parts of the cemetery on a line continued by Taylor's Hill to the west and Folly Path to the east, through what were once local brickworks.

Chapel Row is part of Whinbush Road, named separately to avoid problems with postal numbering. The name appears to arise from its proximity to the Spiritualist Church.

Chapman's Farm Yard* may have been the same as Chapman's Yard, the name illustrating

Bunyan's Dream.

how, up to the nineteenth century, farms were situated in the town rather than in the fields, since the open field system of agriculture meant that one person's holding was in scattered strips rather than in a discrete parcel. *1851*

Chapman's Yard* was one of the slum yards between Queen Street and the river, which were cleared in the 1920s. It was probably named after William Chapman, brewer and licensed victualler who kept the *Peahen* public house in the late nineteenth century. The 1881 census records him as having a domestic servant who was born in the East Indies. *1851, 1861, 1880, 1891, Chapman Yard 1851*

Charlton Road - see Old Charlton Road. *1879*

Churchgate is a shopping development of the 1970s, so called because of its proximity to the Churchyard and parish church. The original proposal was to name it Trinity Way after Trinity College in Cambridge, which was granted the manor of Hitchin Rectory by King Henry VIII in 1547 following the dissolution of the monasteries.

St Mary's Churchyard by Frederick L Griggs.

Church Lane* - see Churchyard and Lyle's Row. *1700, 1844*

Churchyard is part of the ancient graveyard of the parish church. Previously the Churchyard would have been part of the land of the Benedictine monastery dedicated to St. Andrew, founded on this site in 792 by the nobles of King Offa of Mercia. The graveyard may have been larger than can be seen now as burials have been discovered on the far side of Bancroft. Officially, only the western side of the Churchyard now appears to bear this name, the northern and southern sections being called Churchyard Walk, although an 1844 map shows the southern part as Church Lane. *1880, Church Yard 1841, 1851, 1861*

Churchyard Walk - see Churchyard.

Cock Street* - see High Street. *1818, 1841, 1844, 1851*

Cock Yard* was the yard of the *Cock Inn* in Cock Street, now High Street. *1851*

Codpiece Alley* - see West Alley. *1700, Codpisse Alley 1676*

Convent Close is a development of 1979 on the site of a house known as *The Grove*. This became a girls' day and boarding school, established originally by French nuns, the Sisters of the Sacred Heart, in 1907.

Coopers' Alley is now named from its proximity to the *Coopers' Arms* public house but earlier it had probably been known as Queen's Head Passage when the building at its Tilehouse Street end was a public house of that name. Prior to that, part of it is said to have had the name of Pigs Alley.

Corpus Alley* - see West Alley.

Corrie's Yard* - see Exchange Yard. *1841, 1851, 1880*

Crown Yard* was behind the *Crown* public house in Bancroft. *1891*

Davis Alley* lay to the east of Queen Street and no doubt took its name from an owner or tenant. It appears to be the same property as that known sometimes as Grant's Yard which was demolished in 1958. *1861, 1948*

Dead Street* - see Queen Street. *1676, 1700, 1818, 1841, 1844, 1851*

Elmside Walk was laid out as a replacement of the former right of way through the grounds of what is now Hitchin Boys' School. It was named after the house at its southern end, once owned by the Thompson family, one of whose members, Lawson Thompson, was Chairman of the Hitchin Urban District Council for six years until 1909.

Exchange Yard adjoins the Corn Exchange which was built in 1853. It was previously known as Corrie's Yard after John Corrie, a smith, who erected a row of cottages here in 1819, naming them Union Place. A gunsmith, Francis Corrie, who was probably John's son, also lived here at the time of the 1841 census. It is now often referred to as Brooker's Yard after the firm which occupies it. *1899*

Elm Tree by Gerard Ceunis.

Fells Close was built in the early 1980s and is named after John Fells who had market gardens in the Whinbush Road, Nightingale Road and Grove Road area in the nineteenth century. He and his wife, Rebecca, with their family, lived in the appropriately named Gas House at Starlings Bridge as he was also at one time manager of the gasworks there.

Fishponds Road passes what were once enclosed fields, Fishpond Closes, where there was a pond formed by the widening of the Capswell Brook, the tributary of the River Hiz which rises on Butts Close. This is now piped but still flows under the Hitchin Boys' School grounds and Bancroft, joining the river behind the Skynners' Almshouses. The road was laid out at its eastern end in 1907, in what was known as the Bearton Fields Estate, but not completed to Bedford Road until 1920.

Gascoine's Yard* was one of the yards between Queen Street and the river which disappeared in the slum clearances of the 1920s. The 1841 census shows John Gascoine, a victualler, living in Back Street and William Gascoine, a butcher, in Biggin Lane. *1851, 1861, 1891, Gascoin's Yard 1851, 1880*

The Arms of Ralph Skynner.

Gas Path* was a footpath which crossed Benge Mead, now the Bancroft Recreation Ground, from the Skynners' Almshouses to the town's gasworks at Starlings Bridge.

Golden Square* - see Bancroft. *1851, 1861*

Goodwin's Yard* was a yard off Bancroft, named after Samuel Goodwin from Northamptonshire who ran a Classical and Commercial Academy in the main house, living there with his wife, Hannah, and four children, his niece, an assistant, an articled pupil, twelve scholars, and two maids. In addition to being a schoolmaster he also became the clerk to the Local Board of Health. *1851, 1861*

Gorham Place* - see Taylor's Hill. *1851*

Grammar School Walk leads to the school which was re-established in 1889 on this site as

'The Snowfight' by Cyril Pearce,
Art Master 1908-1911

Hitchin Grammar School, having existed since 1639 in Tilehouse Street. Originally the buildings fronting Bancroft were used as schoolrooms, but within a year a new boys' school had been constructed by the Hitchin builder, Matthew Foster. This still exists as the front entrance block seen from the gates.

Grant's Yard* was a yard to the east of Queen Street. It took its name from Daniel Grant, a plumber, decorator and builder who operated from here and who became a deacon of the Bethel Chapel in Bethel Lane in 1881. It may have been the property also known as Davis Alley, but was demolished in 1958 to make way for 'Cannon House' flats.

Gray's Yard* was situated in the lower Hollow Lane area. The 1891 census lists Grays living nearby in both Lyle's Road (Lyle's Row) and Highbury Hill (Kershaw's Hill). *1891*

Green Lane* - see Verulam Road. *1851, 1879, 1883*

Green's Yard* is referred to in 1676 as being off Back Street (Queen Street). Five cottages there were owned by William Brockett alias Green. *1676*

Hall's Yard is a yard to the north of Tilehouse Street, named after William Hall, a grocer, or possibly his father. There still exists an inscription on a wall stating that 'The whole of this wall belongs to W. Hall'. A bottle has been found bearing the name W. Hall, and William's brother, John, was listed as a brewer in 1871. *1841, 1851, 1880*

Harrison Close was built in 1990 on the site of the Hitchin Youth Club. It was named after Colonel John Fenwick Harrison of Kings Walden Bury who had been instrumental in obtaining the land for youth club use in 1944.

Hazelwood Close was developed shortly before the Second World War and is believed to have been so called after someone of this name, rather than a hazel wood.

The Hermitage

Hermitage Road Frederic Seebohm, who occupied the house known as *The Hermitage* in Bancroft, gave part of his garden to allow the road to be constructed in 1875. At one time it was famed for its box trees which were part of the original garden planting. The present buildings were erected on the north side in the late 1920s and on the south mainly in the 1960s. *1879*

Hewitt's Yard* was, no doubt, named after a former owner or occupier.

Highbury Hill* - see Hollow Lane and Whitehill Road. *1879, 1891*

Highbury Road was developed in the late Victorian period but had previously existed as a lane known as Nettle Dell Lane or Road, the land to the north being the Nettle Dell Estate. It has been suggested that the present name was first used by the auctioneers when the estate was divided into building plots. Highbury House had, however, been built here in 1874 and in 1890 George Beaver, a surveyor, wrote that he was widening 'the Highbury road'. The name may suggest that this high land above the town was, in

Trademark of David Greig, Grocer, High Street.

fact, the original site of settlement in a fortified enclosure. *1893, 1900*

High Street is the main commercial street of the town and was, prior to about 1859, known as Cock Street after the *Cock Hotel* which is situated here. Occasionally, it was also considered to be part of Bancroft, of which it is a continuation. *1861, 1880, 1899*

Hitchin Hill is now the uphill road leading southwards from the mediaeval town. The gradient has been eased on at least two occasions by cutting into the hill. The original ground levels can be seen on the footpath to the west which rises to some height above the road. At one time this name was used to refer to the settled area of Stevenage Road at the top of the hill, and there is also a reference to the road being known as Moor Hen Hill after the *Three Moorhens*, an old established public house. *1851, 1883, 1891*

Hollow Lane It is possible that this name is a corruption of Hallow or Holy Lane but, equally, the road drops towards the town in a hollow between two hills. Occasionally, the road appears to have been known as Highbury Hill or Kershaw's Hill. St. Andrew's National School was built here in 1854, and the lower part of the road between St. Andrew's Place and Queen Street came to be called St. Andrew's Street until about 1961. *1676, 1700, 1818, 1841, 1844, 1851, 1880, Holow lane 1556, Hollane 1460*

Honey Lane* was once a road in the mediaeval town but its location is not known. The name probably arose because of its muddy and sticky nature. This is the usual explanation of a similar name in Hertford. *1638*

Hurst's Lane* was once situated off Bancroft, no doubt named after someone called Hurst. *1676*

Kershaw's Hill probably takes its name from the family which operated a coach service from Hitchin to London from 1741 to 1850. Reference can also be found to it being known as Kershaw's Lane and it may be that the name Kershaw's Hill was then being applied to Hollow Lane, with which it runs parallel. The first houses have a date stone inscribed *Telegraph Place 1883* and there are references to it in 1891 as Telegraph Hill and Telegraph Terrace, suggesting that there might once have been a semaphore signalling device set up on the hill, as at Telegraph Hill near Lilley. *1851*

Kershaw's Lane* - see Kershaw's Hill. *1851*

Langford Square* was a yard to the north of Hollow Lane, approximately on the site of Mount Garrison. It could have taken its name from Langford in Bedfordshire, or may be connected with William Langford who was a trustee of the British Schools in Queen Street and is recorded as supplying furniture to local families in 1798. *1851*

Kershaws Coach taken from a painting by W J Shayer in Hitchin Museum.

Love Lane* - see Verulam Road. *1883*

Lower Tilehouse Street - see Tilehouse Street.

Lyle's Row takes its name from George Lyle, an overseer, who erected seven buildings here in 1713. There was also a John Lyle, who seemed to combine a number of parish duties, including schooling, town crying and providing 'a list of the parish duty for the use of the Turnpike Commissioners'. In 1891 this thoroughfare was referred to as Lyle's Row Alley but Drapentier's map of 1700 shows it as Church Lane. *1713, 1841, 1851, 1861, 1880, Lile's Row 1851*

Lyle's Row Alley* - see Lyle's Row. *1891*

Maltmill Lane* was sometimes referred to as Mill Lane and formerly led to Charlton from Tilehouse Street. Its route passed a watermill, the property of the Radcliffe family of the Priory, which was used in the production of malted barley. In a barn in this lane, to the rear of the first houses in Tilehouse Street, Ralph Radcliffe established a school in 1546. It was later used by the Hitchin Vestry as a poorhouse from about 1630 and in 1688 additional property was added to serve as the town's Bridewell or House of Correction. In 1772 the highway was closed by John Radcliffe and the present Old Charlton Road substituted. *1676*

Market Hill* - see Market Place. *1635*

Market Place was the traditional site of the town's market which, no doubt, grew up at the gates of the monastery dedicated to St. Andrew, founded by King Offa's nobles in the year 792 on the site of the present parish church.. It was variously referred to also as Market Hill or Market Square until the present name was confirmed by the Local Board of Health in 1889.

Left and above: *Two views of Hitchin Market by Gerard Ceunis.*

The original market place had been a large triangular widening of Bancroft, bounded by the present Churchyard, Sun Street, Tilehouse Street, Bucklersbury and the High Street but over the centuries it had been encroached on by building, even more so than can be seen today. In 1829 the old Market Bell House, Manor Court House and the Middle Row, all of which were located in this area, were demolished. Later, in the 1850s, a block of butchers' premises in the south-west corner, known as the Shambles, was cleared away. *1700, 1818, 1844, 1851, 1880, 1899*

Market Square* - see Market Place. *1861*

Mill Lane* - see Maltmill Lane. *1700*

Mill Yard* was a yard off Portmill Lane, opposite the watermill. *1851, 1891*

Moor Hen Hill* - see Hitchin Hill.

Moss's Corner* - see Bancroft.

Mount Garrison is cut into the side of Windmill Hill in what may have been a former gravel pit, occupied until the late 1920s by yards and small cottages. The name has survived from the time before any development took place on the site when it was the name of the field, possibly because of its ownership in the eighteenth century by Robert Hinde of Preston, Captain of the Hitchin Militia. *1676, 1819*

Munt's Alley is officially so named because the shop at the High Street end was occupied by Munt's toy and bicycle business until the early

Advertisement for Moss's tea, Hitchin Directory 1948.

1970s. Many local residents know it as Aram's Alley after Eugene Aram, an eighteenth century usher at the church school who was later convicted of a murder and hanged. Edward Bulwer Lytton used Aram's name for one of his novels, although the facts in his story are fictitious. Sometimes the twitchell slightly further north is referred to as Aram's Alley but, whichever it is, his ghost is said to haunt it still.

Nettle Dell Lane* - see Highbury Road. *1851*

Nettle Dell Road* - see Highbury Road. *1900, 1901*

Newstreate* was obviously a new street at one time but its location is now unknown. *1556*

Newton's Way was constructed in the late 1960s to serve the fire station and firemen's houses and is named after Isaac Newton, the superintendent of the Hitchin Fire Brigade from 1815 until 1850. It was his father Robert who, as people's churchwarden, had persuaded the vestry in 1814 to replace the old firefighting equipment with a horse-drawn manual pump operated by ten men. As a result of this action the Hitchin firefighting establishment came into being, lasting until the Second World War, when a National Fire Service was established. There was a family link between the Hitchin Newtons and Sir Isaac Newton, the seventeenth century English scientist.

Nightingale Lane* - see Verulam Road. *1867, 1874, 1878, 1883*

Nightingale Road seems to have been named

Munt's

WELWYN GARDEN CITY	Tel. 395
HIGH STREET, HITCHIN	Tel. 29
EASTCHEAP, LETCHWORTH	Tel. 1678

Advertisement for Munt's stores, 1951.

Isaac Newton from a sketch by Samuel Lucas.

23

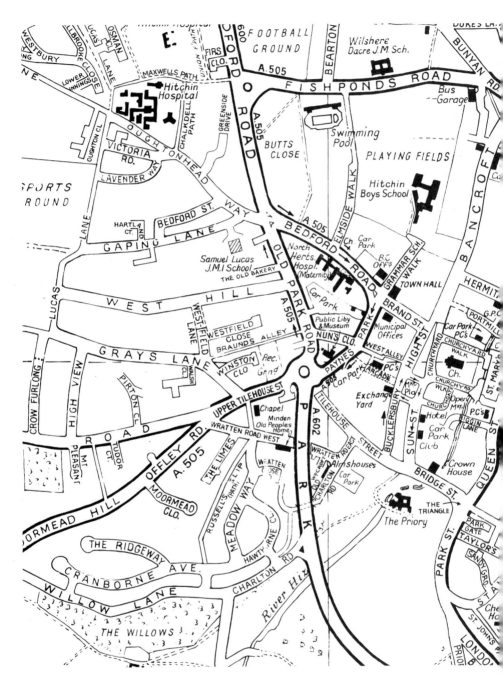

24

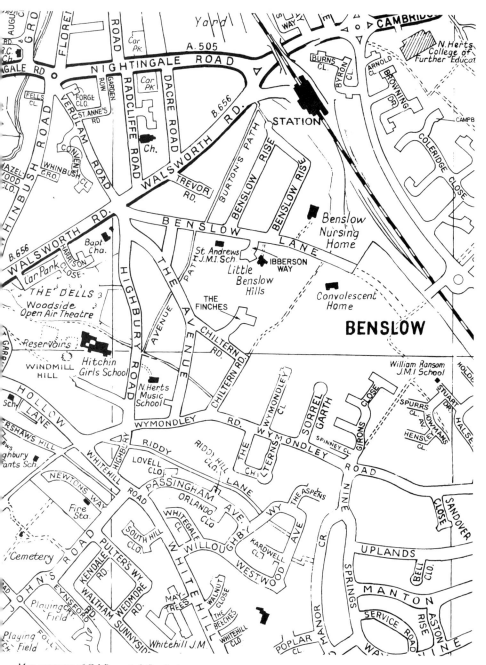

Map courtesy of G I Barnett & Son Ltd

25

after the pair of houses with a date stone inscribed *Nightingale Cottages 1844* which were probably erected on a parcel of land known as Nightingale Close. This, in turn, was possibly so called because such birds were frequently seen there but, equally, may have taken its name from a person. The road may have been that referred to much earlier as the Walwey, being the way to Walsworth from Hitchin. The *Nightingale* public house took its present name from the road, having previously been called the *Leicester Railway Hotel*. Originally the Midland Railway's trains from Leicester reached London by means of the Bedford to Hitchin line, dismantled in the 1960s, then via the Great Northern Railway's tracks to King's Cross. The bridge over the River Hiz is known as Starlings Bridge, probably because the birds are common here although it may be after an earlier property owner in the area. *1861, 1879*

Nuns Close was originally a footpath across a parcel of land known as Payne's Park, and constructed as a road in 1903. It lies on the line of what appears to be an ancient right of way from the church and market via West Alley, Nuns Close, Braund's Alley, Grays Lane and over Gaping Hills, passing Oughton Head on the way to the village of Pirton, which was an important mediaeval settlement. It seems to have been named after the nuns of Elstow Abbey, which held the manor of Hitchin Rectory from the time of King Henry II until the dissolution of the monasteries.

Old Charlton Road was formerly the road to the hamlet of Charlton until Park Way was built, cutting off this short section.

Oldcrosse Waie* was once presumably 'the road leading to the old cross' but it cannot now be identified. *1556*

Old Park Road runs beside the area of land once known as Payne's Park and has also been called Old Park Row and Park Road. *1851, 1879*

Old Park Row* - see Old Park Road. *1844*

Old Storehouse Lane* - see Storehouse Lane. *1844, 1851, 1883*

Bird scarer on roof of Maple Court, Old Park Road.

Parcell's Yard is a yard off Bucklersbury, approached through the present Red Lion Yard. It was probably named after George Parcell who is recorded as living there in 1841, aged 50, of independent means. *1841, 1851, 1880, 1891*

Park Gate is a recent development off Park Street on the site of the former Pierson's Yard. The parkland of the Priory is situated on the opposite side of Park Street, hence the name.

Park Lane* - see Brand Street. *1676*

Park Road* - see Old Park Road. *1888*

One-time school attended by Joseph Lister, Park Street.

Park Street is the road which runs to the east of Priory Park, serving its Kennel Gate, continuing uphill as Hitchin Hill. *1851, 1861, 1880*

Park Way is a relief road for Bridge Street and Tilehouse Street built across Priory Park in the early 1980s.

Paynes Park was originally known as West Lane, the westernmost point of the mediaeval

town. In the nineteenth century it seems to have taken the name from the adjoining parcel of land, Payne's Park. In 1819 one of the trustees of the Free School, Timothy Bristow, complained of an attempt to deprive the school of the use of the field, which it had enjoyed for over seventy years. This was probably at the time that, according to the Vestry minutes, George Kershaw proposed to give up his right to a private road and to consent to its being a public road twenty-five feet wide, from the Free School to newly-built cottages at the north end of the close of pasture formerly called Payne's Park. *Paine's Park 1841, Pains Park 1851*

Peahen Alley* does not appear to be identical to Peahen Yard as both are mentioned in the 1891 census, but it was obviously nearby. *1891*

Peahen Yard* was the yard of the former *Peahen* public house in the lower part of Hollow Lane. *1891*

Penn's Yard* was in the lower Hollow Lane area and was no doubt named after its owner or occupier, who had other properties in the vicinity. *1889, 1891*

Pierson's Yard* was a yard on the site of the present Park Gate and appears to have taken its name from Thomas Gorham Pierson, a local solicitor. There is a reference in the 1851 census returns to 'Mr. Pierson's new houses'. *1861*

Pigs Alley* - see Coopers' Alley.

The solicitor Thomas Gorham Pierson from a drawing by Samuel Lucas

Portmill Lane is the lane in which the Port (or town) Mill was situated on the River Hiz. The

Port Mill, from a sketch by Samuel Lucas.

mill was sold by the Crown in 1813 and rebuilt in 1815 but was acquired by the Local Board of Health in 1852 for demolition to allow the main sewer to be constructed under the bed of the river. *1841, 1851, 1861, 1880, 1891, Port Mill Lane 1676, 1818, 1844, 1851, Portemyll lane 1556*

Portmill Square* Following the demolition of slum properties adjoining Portmill Lane and the later construction of a car park on the site, the Hitchin Urban District Council appears to have referred to the car park by this name, although it does not seem to have officially conferred it on the area.

Post Office Alley* - see West Alley. *1851, 1880*

Pound Lane* - see Brand Street. *1700, 1818*

Priory End The construction of Park Way cut off this short section of Gosmore Road. It was given its present name because of its proximity to Priory Park.

Pulter's Lane* - see Brand Street.

Pump Court* - was a courtyard on the north side of West Alley in which there was a pump providing water for the adjoining cottages.

Quakers' Alley* - see West Alley. *1694, 1841, 1851, 1861*

Queen's Head Passage.

Queen's Head Passage* - see Coopers' Alley.

Queen Street The present name was confirmed in 1889 by the Local Board of Health, although there is evidence of its being known as such earlier. Originally it had been the Back Street of the early town, but after the majority, if not all, of its residents died during the Black Death in 1349 the southern part of it acquired the name of Dead Street. It seems that Queen Street originally replaced this name in the mid-nineteenth century, and soon was extended to the full length of the street. There are brief references to it as Railway Street in the 1880s some years after the railway came to the town, presumably because it led to the station via Walsworth Road, often then called Station Road. *1861, 1880, 1883, 1891*

Railway Street* - see Queen Street.

Rratten Lane* - see Wratten Road East. *1844, 1851, Wratten Lane 1676*

Ratten Road* - see Wratten Road East. *1844, 1851*

Rawling's Hill* - see Windmill Hill. *Rawlins Hill 1676, 1819*

Red Lion Yard* was the yard of the *Red Lion Inn*, a large property situated in the Market Place which was demolished in 1853 for the construction of the Corn Exchange. *1851*

The British Schools, Queen Street.

Red Lion Yard After the demolition of the original *Red Lion Inn* another public house of that name arose in Bucklersbury, with a yard from which several other businesses operated. Although the premises are no longer a public house, the carved lion can still be seen over the present shop front.

Richardson's Alley runs from Sun Street to the yard of the *King's Arms* public house in Bucklersbury and takes its name from William Richardson, the proprietor of the premises in the mid-nineteenth century. *1851*

Riddy Lane was formerly the road from Hollow Lane to the Ippolytts Brook, and has sometimes been called Riddy Road. The brook was often known as The Riddy, from the Old English *riðig*, meaning "little stream", and the lane is sometimes given the same name. A 1676 mention of Riddy Path may also be to this lane. *Ridey Lane 1851*

Riddy Path* - see Riddy Lane. *1676*

Riddy Road* - see Riddy Lane. *1877*

River Side* was a short path on the east bank of the River Hiz north of Bridge Street, originally serving several cottages which faced the river. *1851, 1880*

St. Andrew's Place takes its name from the former St. Andrew's National School which was erected in 1854 at the corner of this road and Hollow Lane. *1861, 1880*

St. Andrew's Street* - see Hollow Lane. *1861, 1891*

St. John's Path takes its name from St. John's Road. When this was known as Bethel Lane the path was Bethel Path.

St. John's Road was formerly known as Bethel Lane after a Bethel Chapel situated there, and when the chapel was replaced by St. John's Church the road was renamed accordingly. The church no longer exists, the Cheshire Home being partly situated on its site.

St. Mary's Square was formed in 1930 following the demolition of slum properties and yards off Queen Street, and takes its name from the parish church across the river. It was intended that buildings of civic importance should be constructed around the square but, apart from the telephone exchange in 1955, this scheme has not come to fruition.

St. Mary's Street* - see Sun Street. *1676, Sainte Marie Streate 1556*

Sandy Grove lies in an area of sand and gravel deposits which have been extensively worked in the past. It was developed by Hilson and Twigden in 1985.

Seamans Yard* Its position is now unknown as is the origin of the name. It is likely that it was named after a person rather than an occupation. 1881

Seymour's Alley* was a small yard to the east of Queen Street which took its name from the Seymour family, local carpenters and builders. *1851, 1861, 1891*

Cemete37ry Gates, St John's Road.

Advertisement, 1899 Handbook to Hitchin

ESTABLISHED 1790.

Wm. Seymour & Son

Builders, Shop Fitters, Blind Makers, Decorators, Painters, &c.

Library Fittings Wall Panellings Cosy Corners Fitments Overdoors Mantels Shop Fittings Show Cases &c., &c.

Reliable Workmanship.   Reasonable Prices.

The latest designs in Wall Papers.
Plain and Decorative Painting at lowest prices.
Estimates and Designs for work in every department submitted.

Wm. Seymour & Son, Queen St., Hitchin.

Seymour's Yard* was, apparently, not the same place as Seymour's Alley as both seem to have been in existence at the same time but was in close proximity to it. It was here that the family firm of carpenters and builders operated, run mainly by William Seymour and his son Frank, although it had existed since 1790 and continued until about 1931 when the family also had a company manufacturing concrete blocks on this site. *1891*

Sheep Market* - see Bancroft. *1861*

Ship Yard* was the yard of the former *Ship* public house in Queen Street. *1861*

Silver Street* - see Bancroft. *1700, 1818, 1844, 1851, 1879, Silverstreate 1556*

Spital Street* or **Spittle Street*** - see Bridge Street. *Spittelstreate 1556, Spittle Street 1676*

Standhill Close is an early 1980s street off Standhill Road, from which it is named.

Standhill Road probably took its name from Standhill Field or Stondelfield, one of the mediaeval open fields of Hitchin. The area is rich in sand and gravel deposits and the name would appear to come from the stone dells or gravel pits which once existed here. Following the opening of the cemetery in 1857 the road was constructed in 1870 at a time of unemployment when a subscription was taken to supplement the highway rate. It was originally known as Cemetery Road, a name which subsequently fell into disuse but was later re-used elsewhere. *Standell Road c 1939*

Starlings Bridge - see Nightingale Road. *1676, 1841, 1851, 1879*

Station Road* - see Walsworth Road. *1882, 1897*

Stonemason's Yard* was occupied by a stone and marble mason, John Warren, but there would appear to have been dwellings there as well. It seems to have been situated next to the British Schools in Queen Street. *1851, 1861*

Storehouse Lane A map reproduced in Frederic Seebohm's book, *The English Village Community,* shows that there was once a storehouse on the eastern side of the lane, although it is not known by whom it was owned or used. The lane has sometimes been referred to, either wholly or in part, as Old Storehouse Lane. *1851, 1880, 1883, 1891*

Sun Street takes its present name from the *Sun Hotel.* Earlier it had been known as Angel Street after the *Angel Inn* which, until it collapsed in 1956, stood on the northern side of the *Sun.* References have been found to it also being called Saint Mary's Street, because it led to the Priory which was dedicated to Our Lady, and possibly even Wearybones Street. *1818, 1841, 1844, 1851, 1880*

Swan Yard* - see The Arcade. *1851*

Taylor's Hill was named after the owner of adjoining land, possibly of the same family as the Taylor of Taylor's Lane (Florence Street). The houses at the top were known as Gorham Place, after Thomas Gorham Pierson, a local solicitor,

Paternoster's former printing office, Sun Street.

who had them built in about 1850. *1851, 1861, 1880. (See map in Appendices)*

Telegraph Hill* - see Kershaw's Hill. *1861*

Telegraph Place* - see Kershaw's Hill. *1883*

Telegraph Terrace* - see Kershaw's Hill. *1891*

The Arcade was originally the yard of the *Swan Inn,* which had existed since at least 1539. In 1884 it was sold to John Gatward, an ironmonger who had adjoining premises, and alterations were made over the years, including glazing over the street end of the yard to form a furniture showroom. In 1927 this was converted to the present shopping arcade, followed shortly afterwards by Arcade Walk, the westward extension.

The Fire Station
The Great Yard.

The Bridgefoot* was probably the area around the bridge in Bridge Street. *1676*

The Great Yard* once existed to the east of the Market Place, behind the *Rose and Crown* public house. It was here that the Hitchin Fire Brigade's engines and firefighting equipment were kept between about 1865 and 1904, when a purpose-built fire station was erected in Paynes Park to celebrate the coronation of King Edward VII. *1851*

The Grenewey* may be identical with Green Lane - see Verulam Road.

The Middle Row* - see Market Place. *1676*

The Riddy* - see Riddy Lane.

The Shambles* - see Market Place.

The Triangle* - see Bridge Street. *1880*

The Walwey* - see Walsworth Road and Nightingale Road. *1460*

Thompson's Yard* was a yard off Paynes Park which no doubt took its name from its owner or occupier. *1861*. There is a modern yard in Tilehouse Street known to some by this name from its occupation by Steve Thompson, a builder.

Thorpe's Alley* took its name from its owner. It was later known as Thorpe's Yard. *1851, 1861*

Thorpe's Yard* - see Thorpe's Alley *1880, 1891*

Tilehouse Street has been, strictly speaking, Lower Tilehouse Street since Park Way cut through it in 1983. It takes its name from the fact that tile kilns once existed at its western end and it has also been referred to as Tylers' Street. The tiled house is a group of existing buildings which were faced with tilehanging in the nineteeth century, long after the street received its name. *1676, 1700, 1841, 1851, 1879, Tile House Street 1818, 1844, 1851, Tylehouse streate 1534, Tylehousestret 1460*

Traveller's Rest Yard* was the yard of the former *Traveller's Rest* public house on the east side of Queen Street. *1861*

Troopers Yard is a yard off Bancroft, given this name in the 1990s when commercial

Coopers' Arms, Tilehouse Street.

The Three Tuns

Former Three Tuns public house, Tilehouse Street.

development took place. The original *Trooper* public house stood at the junction of Bancroft and High Street, later becoming the premises of W.B. Moss and Sons, grocers.

Tyler Street* - see Tilehouse Street. *1851*

Union Place* - see Exchange Yard. *1819*

Verulam Road takes its name from the Roman Verulamium, or St. Albans, probably as a result of the establishment of the diocese of St. Albans in 1877. The name was adopted by the Local Board of Health in 1883 at the request of the Reverend Mr. Gainsford, Vicar of Holy Saviour. It had previously been known as Green Lane, Love Lane or Nightingale Lane. *1882, 1886, 1890, 1891, 1893*

Walsworth Road This is one of the roads from Hitchin to the hamlet of Walsworth which may have once been referred to as the Walwey, the other being Nightingale Road. A map of 1844 shows it as Baldock Road. It had its present name in the middle of the nineteenth century but, following the opening of the railway in 1850, soon became known to many as Station Road. In 1889, however, the Local Board of Health confirmed the name as Walsworth Road. *1851, 1861, 1879, 1880, 1882, 1891, 1893*

Warren's Yard* was yet another yard named after its owner or occupier. Its location would appear to have been in the Kershaw's Hill or Hollow Lane area. In the nineteenth century there were a number of Warrens who all appear to have been stonemasons, in Bridge Street, Dead Street, Highbury and Walsworth Road. *1891*

Wearybones Street* may have been an alternative name for either Bancroft or Sun Street but no explanation is known.

Webb's Yard* was in the lower Hollow Lane area and appears to have been named after Caleb Webb, a grocer and ginger beer manufacturer. *1891*

West Alley was given its present name in 1889 because it led westwards to West Lane. It has, however, enjoyed a number of other names in the past. Originally it may have been known as Corpus Christi Alley, or merely Corpus Alley, which became corrupted to Codpiece or Codpisse Alley. Following the establishment of the Society of Friends' Meeting House here in 1694 it was referred to as Quakers' Alley, then in 1837 the shop at its High Street end became the Post Office and it soon became known as Post Office Alley by some, although still referred to as Quakers' Alley by others.

Dated bricks, West Alley.

West Lane* - see Paynes Park. *1460, 1844, 1851, 1861, 1879*

Whinbush Grove is a short road off Whinbush Road, developed by a builder named George Jeeves between 1856 and 1878. There was at one time a house to the east on the site of Convent Close, known as *The Grove*, which later became a school for girls. *Wimbush Grove 1879*

Whinbush Lane* - see Whinbush Road. *1844, 1861, Wimbush Lane 1851, 1879, 1880, Winbush Lane 1851, 1879*

Whinbush Mews is a small modern development behind older houses in Whinbush

Finial on a house in Whinbush Road.

Road, named in 1997. The word 'mews' originally denoted a place where falcons were kept, later coming to be applied to a stable yard and hence, as in this case, dwellings at the back of others.

Whinbush Road may have been named after the whin or gorse which, presumably, once grew here. The name was officially confirmed in 1889, but the road had earlier been variously referred to as Whinbush, Winbush or Wimbush Lane. A map of 1819 shows Great Wimbush Field lying to the east. *1891*

White Hill* - see Whitehill Road. *1891*

Whitehill Road was probably named after Whitehill Farm or a parcel of land known as Whitehill Piece, in turn so called because of the chalky nature of the earth in the locality. There is, however, a terrace of houses at the top of the hill with a date stone inscribed *Coronation Place Whites Hill 1902*. A map of 1880 shows the section between Hollow Lane and St. John's Road to have been called Highbury Hill, which name was also sometimes applied to Hollow Lane.

Whiting's Yard* formerly existed to the west of the Market Place and was probably named after John Whiting, a fellmonger and 'consistent Quaker'. *1851*

Windmill Hill This short road from Highbury Road serves the properties on the top of the hill. The name comes from the fact that, until it burnt down in November 1875, a windmill stood here known as Rawling's Mill, hence an earlier name for the hill being Rawling's Hill. *1891*

Woodside Gardens is a 1994 development off Walsworth Road. The car park opposite was once the site of a house known as Woodside, sometime the parsonage for Holy Saviour Church.

Wratten Lane* - see Wratten Road East. *1676*

Wratten Road* - see Wratten Road East. *1879*

Wratten Road East consists of the eastern part of Wratten Road which was cut through by the construction of Park Way in 1983. The name is generally considered to have come from the Old English *wrætt*, 'crosswort', and *tun*, 'farm' or 'place', hence a place where crosswort grows. Although not a common plant in Hertfordshire, crosswort has apparently been found abundantly in the Hitchin area. Mid-nineteenth century maps make the distinction between Ratten Road, the east-west section, and Ratten Lane, the north-south Tilehouse Street end.

Crosswort

The Wratten, formerly an early 19th century farmhouse.

41

Acknowledgements

The following people have made invaluable contributions during the compilation of this work and deserve grateful thanks:

Friends at the North Hertfordshire Museum Service for their help and support; the staff at Hitchin Library for their assistance; Alice Dunham, Cilla Dyson and Jill Foot for background information; Jacky Birch for research material, and A. Baxandall Eastham for her major contribution to the text, based on countless hours of research; Bridget Howlett and Terry Knight for help with verifying the text, and proof-reading; George Szirtes, poet, for his prologue; the present-day artists who have enriched the text with their drawings, the major contributor being Daphne Gibson (pages 4, 8, 15, 17, 18, 19, 26, 27, 30, 32, 33, 35, 39, 40) but also Denis B. Dolan (pages 28, 36), Carola Scupham (pages 27, 41), Clarissa Szirtes (title verso and pages 3, 5, 9, 10, 35, 37, 38, 42), Tom Phillips (page 15) and James Willis (page 31); Priscilla Douglas and Pauline Humphries, the tireless production team; David Jones, Tony Handscombe and Dave Bower, technical trouble shooters, and finally, thanks to Nick and Maureen Maddren for their design expertise and to John Street, Terry Dear and the staff of Egon Publishers for their continued help and encouragement.

It has also been a pleasure to use the work of the following well-known Hitchin artists. Gerard Ceunis 1884-1964, Frederick L. Griggs 1876-1939, Samuel Lucas Senior 1805-1870

Roslyn House, Sun Street

Bibliography

The English Village Community, F. Seebohm, Longmans Green & Company, 1883
The History of Hitchin, 2 volumes, R.L. Hine, George Allen & Unwin, 1927 & 1929
The Story of Hitchin, R.L. Hine, Drawings by Gerard Ceunis, William Carling & Company Limited
The Place-Names of Hertfordshire (English Place-Names Society Volume XV), J.E.B. Gover, A. Mawer & F.M. Stenton, Cambridge University Press, 1938
The Concise Oxford Dictionary of English Place-Names, 4th Edition, E. Ekwall, Oxford University Press, 1960
The Book of Hitchin, A.M. Foster, Barracuda Books Limited, 1981
Market Town: Hitchin in the Nineteenth Century, A.M. Foster, Hitchin Historical Society, 1987
The John Mattocke Boys, J. Donald, 1990
Discovering Hitchin, P. Douglas & P. Humphries, Egon Publishers Limited, 1995
The House that Bartlett Built, edited by P. Douglas & P. Humphries, Hitchin Historical Society, 1996
Maps and records in Hitchin Museum, Hertfordshire County Record Office and the Public Record Office
Auction particulars in private collections

The Hitchin Historical Society
The Society, founded in 1977, currently has over 300 members and arranges meetings and visits relating to the history of Hitchin, Hertfordshire, and more general aspects of the study of local history as well as encouraging individual research.

Listed Buildings

In 1909 a Royal Commission on Historical Monuments was set up to make an inventory of all ancient and historical constructions and its report for Hertfordshire was published in 1910. After the Second World War the Ministry of Housing and Local Government was given the statutory duty of compiling lists of buildings of architectural or historic interest to which special protection would be applied in respect of rebuilding or redevelopment work.

Listed buildings with statutory protection are graded into three categories:
Grade I for the very best, comprising only 1% of all listed buildings and
Grade II for the remainder, of which about 4% are given an additional 'star' rating as being particularly special.

Bancroft

Nos. 2 to 5 (consecutive) II
Nos. 6 to 8 (consecutive) II
Nos. 12 to 14 (consecutive) II
Nos. 15 & 16 II
No. 17 II
No. 21 II
No. 21A II
No. 22 II
Nos. 23 & 24 II
No. 25 II
Nos. 26 & 27 II*
Nos. 27A & 28 II

No. 30 II
Nos 32 & 33 II
No. 34 II
Nos 38 to 40 (consecutive) II
Nos. 45, 46 & 46A II
No. 47 II
No. 53 II
Nos. 68 to 83 (consecutive)
(Skynners' Almshouses including the wall and gateways) II
Nos. 86 & 87 II

Nos. 91 & 92 II
No. 93 II
Nos. 95 to 98 (consecutive) II
No. 99 *(Orford Lodge)*
No. 101 II
Nos. 102 & 102A II
Nos. 103 & 103B II
Nos 105 & 106 II
Nos. 107A & 107B II
Nos. 108 & 109 II
No. 121 II

Bedford Road

Thomas Bellamy House II

Council Offices
(former Friends' Meeting House) II

Biggin Lane

The Biggin II*

Brand Street

Nos. 6A & 6B II

Council Offices *(Old Town Hall)* II   Former Library II

Bridge Street

Nos. 8 & 9 II
No. 27 II
No. 29 II

Nos. 30 & 30A II
Nos. 31 & 32 II*

No. 35 II
Nos. 36 to 38 (consecutive) II

Bucklersbury

Nos. 2 & 2A II
Nos. 3 & 4 II
No. 5 II
Nos. 7 & 8 II
Nos. 9 to 12 (consecutive) II
No. 13 II
No. 15 II
No. 16 *(The King's Arms)* II

Nos. 17 & 18 II
No. 19 II
Nos. 20 to 22 (consecutive) II
No. 23 II
No. 24 II
Nos. 25 & 26 II
Nos 27 & 27A II

No. 28 *(part of The Red Hart)* II
No. 29 *(part of The Red Hart)* II*
Nos. 30 & 31 II
Nos. 32 & 32A II
Nos. 33 & 34 *(The George)* II*
No. 37 II
Nos. 39 & 40 II

Churchyard

Church of St. Mary I II
Nos. 1 & 1A II
No. 4 II
No. 5 II

Nos. 6 & 7 II
Nos. 8 to 10 (consecutive) II
No. 11 II

No. 14 II
No. 15 II
Nos. 24 to 28 (consecutive) II

Grammar School Walk

Hitchin Boys' School II

High Street

No. 1 II
No. 2 II
Nos. 3 & 4 II
Nos. 5 & 6 II

No. 8 *(The Cock)* II
No. 17 II
No. 19 II
No. 20 II

No. 21 II
No. 22 II
No. 26 II

Hitchin Hill

The Three Moorhens II

Market Place

Nos. 2 & 2A II
No. 4 II
No. 5 II
Nos. 8 & 9 II*

No. 20 II
No. 21 II
Nos. 22 & 23 II
Nos. 24 & 25 II

Nos. 26 & 27 II
No. 27A II
No. 30 II
No. 32 *(The Corn Exchange)* II

Nightingale Road

Nos. 1 to 4 (consecutive) *(Frythe Cottages)* II

Old Park Road

Nos. 5 to 7 (consecutive) II

Park Street

No. 1 *(Lord Lister Hotel)* II   No. 2 II

Paynes Park

No. 2 *(Paynes Park House)* II   Hitchin Museum II   No. 2A II

Portmill Lane
Nos. 7 & 8 II

Priory Park
The Priory I   Coach House II
Garden Bridge II   Stables II

Queen Street
No. 40 II   Lancasterian Hall *(British Schools)* II*   No. 42 *(Mistress's House)* II
Galleried Classroom   Other British Schools buildings II   Nos. 66 to 68 (consecutive) II
  (British Schools) II*   No. 41 *(Master's House)* II

Sun Street
No. 4 *(The Sun Hotel)* II*   Nos. 10 & 11 II   No. 24 II
No. 5 *(Conservative Club)* II   Nos. 13 & 14 II   Nos. 25, 25B & 26 II
No. 6 II   No. 15 II   Nos. 27 & 28 II
No. 7 II   Nos. 16 & 17 II   Nos. 29 & 30 II
No. 8 II   No. 18 II   Nos. 31 & 32 II
No. 9 II   Nos. 19 & 20 II   Nos. 33, 33A & 33B II

Tilehouse Street
Nos. 1 & 2 II   No. 21 II   Nos. 77 & 78 II
Nos. 3 & 3A II   Nos. 22 to 24 (consecutive) II   Nos. 81 & 82
Nos. 4 & 5 including railings II   Nos. 25 & 26 II   *(The Coopers' Arms)* II*
No. 6 II   No. 27 II   No. 83 II
Nos. 8 to 10 (consecutive) II   No. 28 II   No. 84 II
Tithe Barn behind No. 8 II   No. 29 II   No. 85 II
Nos. 11 & 12 II   No. 30 II   No. 87 II
No. 13 II   Nos. 31 & 32 II   No. 88 II
No. 14 II   No. 35 *(Western House)* II*   No. 89 II
Nos. 15 to 17 (consecutive) II   No. 36 II   No. 94 II
No. 19 II   No. 70 II   No. 95 II
No. 20 II   Nos. 71 to 75 (consecutive) II   No. 96 II

Walsworth Road
No. 1 II

Wratten Road East
Wratten Cottage II

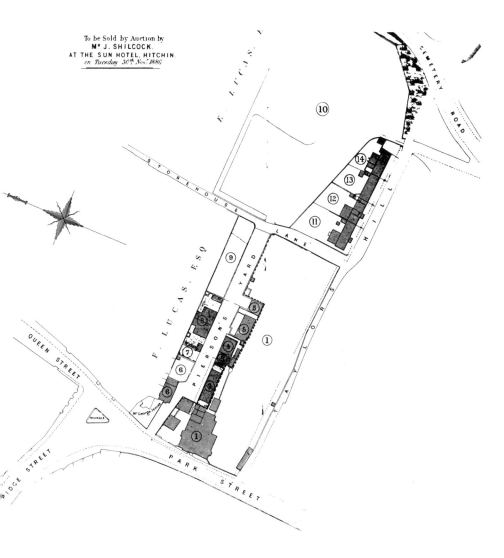

To be Sold by Auction by
Mr J. SHILCOCK.
AT THE SUN HOTEL, HITCHIN.
on Tuesday 30th Nov. 1886.

*Map of Pierson's Yard accompanying auction
details, 1886 (courtesy of Hitchin Museum).*

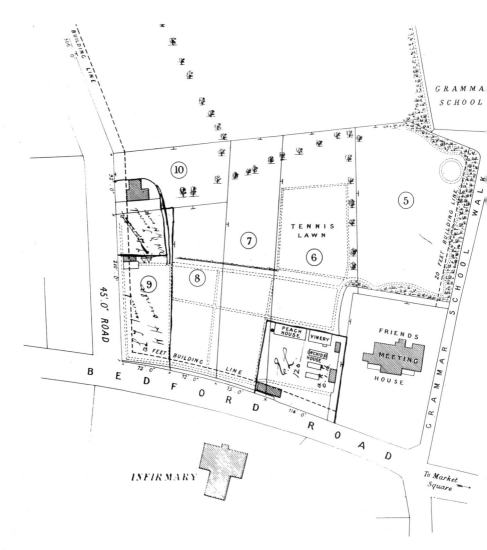

*Plan of building land at Hitchin belonging to the
executors of James H Tuke sold by auction in
May 1896. (Courtesy Hitchin Museum).*